April's Amazing Adventure

Written By: Joanna DeLuca

Published by SAVVY Kids in collaboration with RoseDale Communications
www.CraftingYourMessage.com

Graphics by: Papande Newman
www.newmandesign.info

Foreword

One day a tiny white fur ball was saved by a kind stranger who brought her to the shelter. A baby kitten with no name was quickly named April, in honor of Animal Cruelty Prevention month, by the shelter staff. This was the beginning of April's journey. Her life started out very sadly, but her story didn't end here.

The author fell in love with April's first photo on Facebook and was able to meet her at a fundraiser where she held the baby kitten for the first time in the palm of her hand. She continued to follow April's journey of recovery at the shelter where the kitten was receiving medical care.

April became the luckiest kitten when she was adopted by the author and her husband. They will tell you it was one of their luckiest days. It's been two years since this little kitten was brought to the shelter.

Since that time April has become a celebrity with her own Facebook page. She is thriving as a grown-up cat who loves to hang out with her human family and her kitty sisters. April is an amazing example of what "love" can accomplish.

In the words of the author...

"Your love for all creatures, the great & the small, will always bring good things to you all in all."

Dee Ford,

Board President, SPCA Suncoast

http://www.suncoastspca.org

Dedication

My deepest gratitude to Merribeth and Louis for picking up April off the street and taking her to the SPCA Suncoast in time to save her life.

I am forever thankful to the staff and volunteers at the SPCA Suncoast whose hard work and dedication blessed me with the gift of April the cat.

April and I appreciate all the people, all over the world, that have followed, prayed for & loved her since that first photo on Facebook. Your love has brought her to where she is today.

This is the story
of April the cat.
She had a rough start,
here's more about that.

It happened on
one sad March day,
she was thrown from a car,
just tossed away!

Two kind people saw this
and knew they must help her,
so they jumped in the car
and rushed to the shelter.

The shelter helpers saw her
and just wanted to cry.
We must work quick
so this baby doesn't die!

They cleaned her up

and the vet checked her out.

She was a very sick girl,

of which there's no doubt.

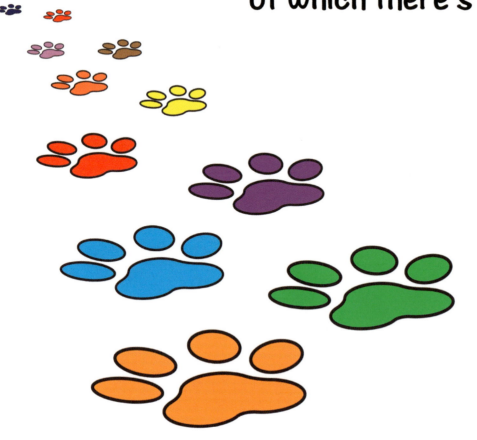

So tiny and frail

at only three weeks old,

it didn't look good

if the truth be told.

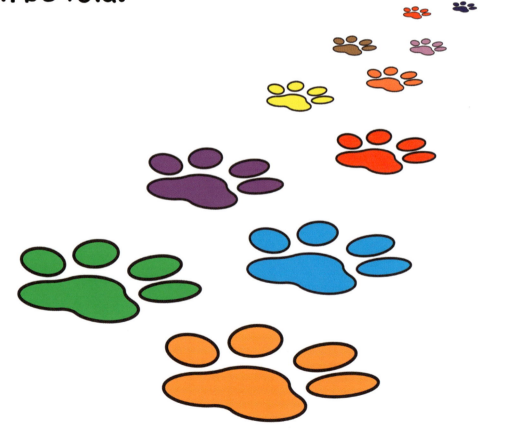

With medicine and food
and lots of tender loving care,
she was posted on Facebook
for all to share.

And share they did,

from far and near,

the outpouring of love

for this little dear!

At first we were amazed
that she was alive,
but then we were excited
as we watched her grow and thrive!

The shelter would post
a weekly "April Update."
All over the world,
we just couldn't wait!

She was getting better,

it was such a thrill!

Looks like from now on,

it's all downhill.

The time had come
to find her a family.
After three months of care,
she would be missed terribly.

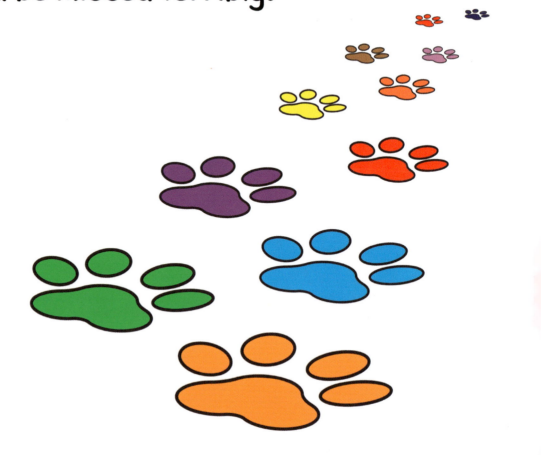

A home was found
with so much love to give.
This sweet little girl
will have a great life to live.

All over the world,

people still love to see,

how she grows and thrives,

this little kitty.

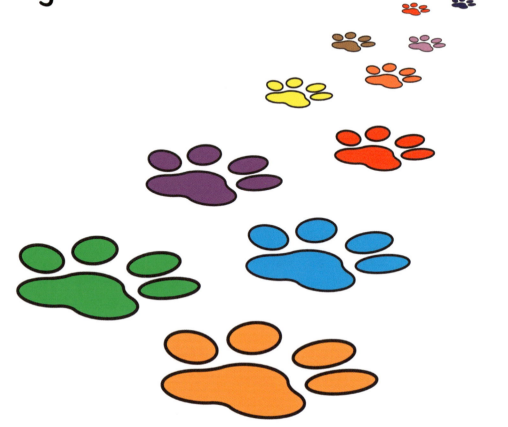

April's Page

Jan 24 at 8:26am · Pasco, Florida ·

Took this yesterday. She just looked so pretty & perfect to me. Of course moved right after I took it.

April's happy today,

and she wants you to know,

that kindness to all

is a great way to show

your love for all creatures,

the great and the small,

will always bring good things

to you all in all.

Our Pledge to April

We, the

_____

family,

promise to be loving to all,

and kind to every creature,

the great and the small.

About the Author

Joanna has been a "crazy cat lady" since childhood. Married with three fur babies, she is a hairstylist by trade. Since adopting April, she serves as a member of the board for the SPCA Suncoast, who were responsible for saving April.

April was horribly neglected as a tiny kitten. Her abuse ended when she thrown from a car at only three weeks old. And then a miracle happened! She was picked up from the side of the road, brought to the SPCA, nursed back to health, and placed with a loving family!

Joanna believes the miracle of April has a purpose and wishes all animal cruelty could have a happy ending. She wrote this book for parents and caretakers to use as a tool to teach children to be kind to animals and stop others from abusing them. Not all animals are as lucky as April.

Joanna desires to make a change and wants to see a world with less and less animal abuse. She believes that teaching children that cruelty is unacceptable is a great start.

Keep your eyes open for more "Adventures of April."

Let April know that you like her book on Facebook at April's Page, @AprilTheCat

Joanna DeLuca with April - Photo by: Lisa Fitch

92289221R00024

Made in the USA
Columbia, SC
26 March 2018